BLUFF YOUR WAY AT BIRDWATCHING

STEVEN SONSINO

RAVETTE BOOKS

Published by Ravette Books Limited
3 Glenside Estate, Star Road
Partridge Green, Horsham
West Sussex RH13 8RA
(0403) 710392

Series Editor – Anne Tauté

Cover design – Jim Wire
Typesetting – Input Typesetting Ltd.
Printing & Binding – Cox & Wyman Ltd.
Production – Oval Projects Ltd.

The Bluffer's Guides are based on
an original idea by Peter Wolfe.

A note on size: In their wisdom, the publishers have decided to make this book – like all the others in the Bluffer's Guide series – just the right size to fit the jacket pocket or handbag. This makes them ideal for easy reference in dangerous situations, such as in the lounge at the George & Dragon, Cley-next-the-Sea, or downstairs at the Porthcressa on St. Mary's in the Isles of Scilly. It also makes a handy midge swatter if you find yourself at the RSPB's Minsmere reserve.

CONTENTS

THE AUTHOR

Steven Sonsino was drawn into the bird-watching web by his birdwatching wife and her fanatical family. His brother-in-law, for example, spent last year abroad, technically, as a language student in Portugal. In reality, he was commuting each weekend between the plains of Spain and the Outer Hebrides looking for birds.

Jackie Sonsino isn't a bad little birder, either, but her husband wishes he knew in 1984 what he knows now. In 1984 an exhausting spring fortnight was spent in Austria. 'It's cheaper in spring', his wife explained, 'after the ski-ing season is over, but before the summer season starts.' What he didn't realise was that she wanted to witness the spring passage of passerine warblers, grubby brown things the size of your little finger, moving north between the Austrian alps. Her idea of a nice little holiday meant trekking halfway across Bavaria, over gigantic mountain ranges. The trip was not a huge success. He slid down one still-slushy ravine on his bottom, all for a closer view of a Ring Ouzel, a Blackbird with white bits on it. Writing this book was his revenge.

His British life-list now stands at well over 800, he claims, but does not include a Tree Sparrow. Although keen to make every effort to be seen trying to see birds, the author would like to make it plain that – being sensitive to the powerful combination of choppy seas and the smell of chum – he has absolutely no intention whatsoever of taking a pelagic trip south of Scilly.

To those long-suffering partners, spouses and colleagues who must cope with the wistful gaze out of the window when it's raining, the angry snarl when asked what sort of weekend was had, and the enormous telephone bill, this book is respectfully dedicated.

INTRODUCTION

What is Birdwatching?

Birdwatching – or birding as true bluffers must call it – is an area that many people know a little about. Of course, the inexperienced birdwatching bluffer can be detected at a glance, simply from what they wear (indescribable), what they say (inappropriate), and where they carry their spare tin of Thornproof dressing.

Some authorities suggest that the prime definition of a birdwatching bluffer (Latin name: *Bluffus bestyoucan*) is one who knows the names of all the birds on the British birdlist, but not how to identify them. True bluffers would certainly not dream of stooping to the level of actually identifying birds – far too much effort is involved.

After months of copious note-taking and surreptitious sound recordings – naturally, of birders, not birds – we conclude that the first step towards becoming a bird bluffer is, quite simply, knowing the jargon. So an important part of your expertise is to use the correct words and phrases to exude an atmosphere of confidence and competence on all matters ornithological.

For instance, you will almost certainly need to know how to differentiate between a twitcher and a dude in the field. One surefire method is that dudes always carry a field guide around to help identify any birds they see. Twitchers, of course, know all the birds and have no need to carry such a book.

Important additions to the wardrobe – what to wear if you had the money and where to be seen in it – need also be covered.

Making lists is a crucial task. To give some idea of how important lists are, consider that Britain's premier charity, The Royal Society for the Protection of Birds (founded 1889, membership half a million), prints, in tiny type, ten identical lists of the birds that regularly – or even occasionally set foot in this country. It also includes those that simply fly over on their way to somewhere more interesting.

An example of the enormity of the task facing you is that of the 500-odd birds on the British list, perhaps half are no larger than five inches from beak to tail and almost impossible to tell apart. They are all buffish-brown, or brownish-buff; some are even greenish yellow, or yellowish green, depending on who describes them. Others have so-called 'identifying characteristics', such as wingbars and eyestripes. Ignore all claims of such things: they are almost impossible to find if the bird has any sense and sits quietly in a suitably-camouflaged tree or bush. Some birds – such as Ringed Plovers and Little Terns – can't even be seen though they nest in the open; what chance have you got when they hide?

A note on size: A bird's size is measured from the tip of its beak or bill to the tip of its tail, and you can only measure this accurately when it is dead and stretched out. Normally when they're wet and huddled on a branch, birds look much smaller than they really are. As a point of reference, the smallest British birds, the Goldcrest and Firecrest, are about 3.5 inches long, so don't make the mistake of reporting a tiny bird of an inch or two to a crowd of birdwatchers in the local hostelry. It just won't wash.

Needless to say, one can't go round with an air rifle taking pot shots at birds just to see how big they are . . . or were. (Though this doesn't seem to deter some Europeans.) In any case, the British tradition is to make rough guesses as to size, largely to prolong the identification process. Accurate measurements would somehow spoil the fun.

Pecking Order

It is essential to recognise the pecking order (pun intended) of the various groups and individuals that make up the birdwatching world.

Near the top are the birdwatching agencies and conservation groups, including the Royal Society for the Protection of Birds and the Wildfowl Trust. It is difficult to believe that the formation of the RSPB was prompted a century ago by women's hats. However, 19th century fashions caused the formation of a female pressure group bent on preventing the slaughter of Egrets and other avian exotica for the millinery trade.

The other big conservation group is The Wildfowl Trust, brainchild of Sir Peter Scott, son of the famous Scott of the Antarctic, and perhaps the world's best known bird artist of recent years. From small beginnings in 1946 at Slimbridge in Gloucestershire, the Trust has now added six more major reserves across Britain. Apart from enabling thousands of bluffers to practise on other bluffers by collecting and concentrating birds and birders from all over the country in seven locations, the Trust has introduced the amazing Adopt-a-Duck, Support-a-Swan and Foster-a-Flamingo schemes. Bluffers are recommended to join as it places you in a sympathetic light when the fact is 'accidentally' revealed in public.

The conservation agencies are closely followed by the clothing and equipment manufacturers. Then come the top bird information suppliers, some of whom happen to be Britain's top birders. These birders share one important characteristic: they make money out of telling other birders where to find the particular things they need to add to their lists.

There is also the Bird Information Service in King's Lynn, Norfolk, which runs Birdline – a telephone service that informs the listener (at breakneck speed) which road to park in, in which county, which fence to climb, and which bush to look for to see a Parula Warbler.

Besides these are the speciality book publishers, and certain pages on Ceefax and Oracle that give information on British rarities, but which have a habit of being out of date very quickly, so are best used on Saturday when they've been renewed for the week.

You also need to know that Eric Simms is the hero of the birding world. Besides making innumerable recordings of bird calls and song, sometimes apparently from the most dangerous of positions, he has written a splendid series of books about life in Dollis Hill, his favourite London suburb, and his trips by bicycle to Staines Reservoir at unearthly hours in the morning. By quoting the odd passage verbatim in any conversation, bluffers are bound to enhance their reputation. Especially if they know how to find Staines Reservoir without using the M25.

Lastly come the birds themselves. Because no self-respecting bluffer would spend hours in the cold, soaked to the skin, trying to establish whether some bedraggled walnut was a common or garden Greenish Warbler or a Two-barred Greenish Warbler, you should concentrate on easy to see birds. If you are tempted to try real birdwatching, there is one simple piece of advice we can give: don't. The best sightings of 1988's Little Bustard in the New Forest – its first visit to Britain for over 12 years – were made by millions of viewers in the comfort and warmth of their own homes. When birdwatchers first found the bird, a drab female, cowering in the undergrowth, they flushed it out for what they thought would be a better view. It emerged on the opposite side from them, and rather thoughtfully flew directly over the BBC's Nine O'Clock News team, who filmed it flying off into the distance. The sodden birdwatchers had to walk twenty miles to find it again before dark.

THE BLUFFER PREPARES

Types of Birdwatcher

It is important to realise that there are actually several recognised (and recognisable) categories of birdwatcher. Serious birdwatchers prefer to be called birders. Apparently it sounds more active than birdwatching. This makes a little more sense when one considers the speed with which certain individuals fly – often literally – from one end of the country to the other, for the sake of a possible Red-eyed Vireo.

One grade up from the birder is the twitcher. No-one is quite certain of the reason for the name, but the consensus is that they either twitch with excitement when they hear news of a rarity, or that they twitch off to different parts of the country at the drop of the hat. In the old days, it used to be quite difficult to be a twitcher: first, one never heard what was about, unless you were a member of the select grapevine, and second, one had to hold one's job. Now, with so many unemployed, twitching is much easier as it readily fits in around signing on days.

More dedicated and less tactful than twitchers are the maniacs, who sleep, drink, eat and talk nothing but birds. It sounds like a pleasant and harmless enough pastime, but when you consider that these people generally sleep rough, eat badly and make appalling conversation, maybe you should decide it isn't worth it. Some maniacs actually have homes, but have forgotten where they are. Many of them refuse to drive on the off-chance that they will see something in the skies.

Lastly somewhere in the rarefied atmosphere of the higher echelons of bird life, are the ornithologists. These people are actually paid, mostly to collect, weigh and analyse bird droppings, or guano, but it's terribly important work and gets published in deep and meaningful academic tomes, all of which can quite safely be ignored.

The most serious mistake a bluffer can make is to call a birder a dude. It doesn't matter if you call maniacs dudes. You won't be around long enough afterwards to tell the tale.

Dudes are often characterised in the field by red kagouls or fluorescent anoraks to let the birds know they're coming. Another feature of the dude is the ever-present field guide, a book that identifies all the birds you're ever likely to see in one sitting (and then some). This they constantly refer to, even in hides, which is frowned upon in general as it lowers the tone, and spoils the fun of trying to establish what's what without any help. Helping a twitcher identify a bird is usually to be avoided, but there could be a case for arguing that a helpful bluffer might do so, in an attempt to pull rank.

Dudes do, however, know some things about birds, and appear to be excellent at RSPB quizzes.

Below dudes, comes another category of birdwatcher, perhaps it could even be a sub-class of dudes: greenies. These are embryonic bluffers without the advantage of having read this book. They wear all the right (green) gear, have all the right equipment, but as soon as they open their mouths and say 'Excuse me, do you know what that little brown wader might be?' you know they're true greenies. The most galling thing about greenies if you are a birder is that they almost always have better 'scopes and bins, as the bluffer must call telescopes and binoculars. However, one of the unwritten rules of the hides and byways is: 'Thou shalt not look through any other piece of equipment but thine own – unless someone offers first.'

Bird spotter and bird fancier as names (general, for the use of) are – quite simply – not used.

Equipment

To be outstanding in their own field, practising bluffers must be seen in the right clothes. We'll start from toe to top.

Boots

The bluffer aiming at the birder or twitcher level should wear very old wellingtons, preferably ones that look as though they leak. The weekend bluffer, quite happy to be a dude, or even a greenie (if you absolutely must), should go for an expensive pair of walking or hiking boots.

The key things to look for when buying walking boots are not – as one might suppose – the quality of the foxing (a layer of rubber above the sole to protect the leather) or the effectiveness of the Cambrelle lining in keeping you dry if you step in a pond, but the pair with the most exotic, even macho, name. And, whenever possible, the pair that costs as much as you can possibly afford, or – better still – twice as much.

Top recommended boot names are as follows:

Zamberlan Trek-Lites – mention the bellows tongue in passing and amaze your friends;

Scarpa Trionic Manta Attak – these make a useful combination with Yeti gaiters;

Raichle Sporty 2 – with user-friendly laces.

If you aren't prepared to take a second mortgage to pay for your boots, the next best thing is to buy a pair of trainers for £6.99 from somewhere like Freeman Hardy & Willis. Do ensure they have something quite inappropriate emblazoned on the tongue or round the heel. 'Squash' trainers work well, as do those marked 'Badminton'.

Waxed jackets or Waterproofs

A famous climber once reported that there was no such thing as good or bad weather, only good or bad clothing. Bad clothing is, of course, relative – any coat at all has to be better than none, especially in places such as Aberystwyth and Manchester, where it rains continuously – but as far as birding is concerned 'bad' really translates as 'multi-coloured kagouls', or anoraks, as worn by dudes.

Greenies, on the other hand, have the right idea. They tend to wear waterproof, or better still waxed, jackets and coats from the most expensive suppliers. However, in attempting to keep their coats in pristine condition, greenies won't usually resort to covering their jackets with badges and sew-on labels, which is an essential feature of the twitcher's wardrobe.

If you want to use a waterproof jacket – and there is little else you can wear in the rain that will keep you dry (short of resorting to a tent on wheels) – then you could always buy a navy-coloured coat. This colour is only now becoming fashionable, and it's bound to take a year or two before sales begin to accelerate. So we would suggest that, if you are in the market for a water and windproof jacket, blue would do. (It also has the advantage of automatically excluding you from the growing category of greenies.)

Besides the two most important aspects of waterproof clothing – colour and cost, in that order – there is the strange question of pockets. Most birders only ever find half the pockets in their coats in a lifetime, and a good third of these are never used. The reason is quite simple, but sometimes disturbing to the unseasoned or vegetarian bluffer: dead animals.

The waterproof coat was originally sold as a huntin', shootin', fishin' jacket, but has fairly recently become standard issue for the birder. A great deal of motorcyclists' Belstaff jackets have also been subverted to the cause and these are quite credible, especially in large crowds ranged round newly-landed rarities on a fresh Spring morning at St. Abbs Head, near Berwick on Tweed. They do smell a bit, though, especially if you're crammed into a tiny, two-person hide along the banks of Cambridgeshire's Old Bedford River at Welney's Wildfowl Refuge.

A few things to look out for when buying waterproof jackets:

Kangaroo pockets: when running for the ferry, or racing to catch the mailboat bound for Fair Isle, these pockets, wide across the chest, have a tendency to bounce vigorously, creating the effect of a hopping birder. (Depending on where the pocket is, the effect of the bouncing can be quite painful . . . to either sex.)

Beard flap: especially designed for naturalists, this piece of material folds across the inside of the zip to prevent the teeth snagging or digging into the neck. These can be difficult to zip up without taking the hood off, or without a helping hand from a friend.

Poacher's pocket: some people are able to store their scopes in here together with volumes 1 to 3 of *Birds of the Western Palearctic*, so they're quite big.

Storm pockets: never keep a notebook or any other essential item in these. The system of triple or even quadruple locking – with zips, flaps, tags and tie-strings – makes easy access a virtual impossibility.

Goretex: a fabric that allows you to breathe instead of suffocate. (A material with a future, this one.)

Ultrafleece: a brushed synthetic material that's wind-proof and hard-wearing: not what happens to you when you buy all the necessary clothing in one go.

Headgear

The most essential item of clothing any birder can have is a bobble hat, preferably self-knitted, in the most garish colours possible. Matching gloves earn you an extra point.

Bins

Having dressed for the part, the first real piece of hardware you need is a pair of bins, binos, binocs or binoculars. Some pairs of bins have rubber eye pieces, some don't. Some of them fold back (to allow spectacle users to get a close-up), others don't. In fact, the question of bins is entirely subjective, so it's easy for the bluffer to pontificate forcefully on almost any brand or type. Do not let the numbers (7x50, 10x40, etc.) phase you. The small number refers to the magnification given by the small end of the bins, the end you look through. You need anything between 7 and 10 really. The big number tells you how big the big bits are at the front in millimetres. Don't buy anything bigger than 50, and nothing smaller than 20. (The only use for Opera glasses is Opera.)

There is a series of clever calculations you can do to ensure the bins aren't diddling you out of too much light, but it is an extremely confusing test, and best ignored by bluffers. ('Oh, I don't bother with those; if it has the right feel, that's all that matters . . .')

Another essential item is the useful, all-purpose eyepiece cover – this keeps the rain off the eyepieces and conveys the impression of the hard-weather birder, fit for the next easterly gale.

When you finally get a pair of bins out in the field, scuff them up a bit, take off the case and throw it away – no one uses their case to store bins. You never know, too, what lighthearted banter might be struck up by sticking badges or labels over your bins. NB: Do not stick badges over the big round lenses at the front of your bins. It tends to obscure the view.

If you have a birding partner be sure to buy two pairs of bins: sharing them is a real problem. Also try to make sure you get a pair of roof prism bins. It isn't necessary to know their pros and cons, but it is the current industry buzzword.

List of bins: Leica, Leitz, Swift, Zeiss, Zeiss.
(This is not a misprint, there are two Zeiss's: from East and West Germany.)

Telescopes and Tripods

The next piece of kit to work for is the telescope. These are much more expensive and cost from £200 upwards. They do however distinguish the bluffer from the vast majority of dudes, who don't have 'scopes. However, there is the danger of confusion with greenies, who tend to have a little more disposable income.

A useful ploy, if you can't afford a permanent 'scope, is to contact a mail-order manufacturer, ask if you can borrow a 'scope on a month's free-trial, then send it back before the month is up and start again. In this way, bluffers can extract the maximum birding time with a 'scope for the minimum amount of money.

Telescope suppliers tend to have the word Opto- or Opti- in their name and quite a few have the letter K in there somewhere. Typical examples of the latter include Kowa, Adlerblick and so on. Don't worry about B, Z or G numbers in model numbers, but always argue that B is best.

Tripods

Tripods are used for holding telescopes off the ground. They can be adapted to suit birders of different heights, which is quite useful. Most of them have three legs, but some of them only have one, when they're known as monopods. These generally cost about a third as much as a tripod, but don't stand up on their own, which is why so many 'scopes these days are decorated with green rubber: to cushion the bounce. There are also short, table top tripods which can be used in hides with shelves, but the best form of telescope support in a hide is the window clamp, or mount, which screws to the edge of the window, either in a hide or in the car. It can also be used as an instrument of torture on the hide chatterer. There's always one.

Bird Photography

If you have a tripod and a telescope you're half way to becoming a bird photographer. However, the really effective photographic bluffers have a camera, too, which they attach to the tripod. A big and heavy telephoto lens is absolutely necessary if you want to impress in this arena – 1000mm is the norm; what this actually refers to is not important. Photographic bluffers can, however, show a little bit of knowledge in the presence of other non-photographic birders by muttering about f-numbers and generally disparaging the lighting conditions.

Recording Birdsong

Using a simple tape recorder to capture birdsongs and calls is almost pointless. You'll record more of your own rustlings than anything else. Some machines have recording gun microphones that focus in on a particular winged singer, but cut out a good deal of extraneous sound. The serious recordist will obtain as big a parabolic dish as possible and fit the microphone into the middle of it. Eric Simms is of course the master of this art, but H.F. Witherby, Ludwig Koch and James Fisher are also names worth dropping.

Lists

Lists are of prime importance to the bird world, and the bluffer should be ready to reel off sightings and dates from those lists at any moment. The only list really worth bothering about is the official British list, as compiled by the British Ornithological Union, although each county has its own list of regulars, accidentals and vagrants, too.

Bluffers should also maintain a permanent mental record of their British life list total, i.e. the number of birds they have seen since the day they were born; and of their back garden list, the birds they have seen in or from their back garden.

The difficulty most bluffers have with life lists is knowing exactly where to pitch them, but here's a rough rule of thumb guide:

British life list tally	Birding status
0–10	EEC politician
11–75	Greenie
76–200	Dude
201–450	Birder
451+	Maniac

Of course, there is a degree of overlap, particularly at the extremes of the list, but on the whole the division is fair. There are dangers, though, in pitching one's life list too high; it is possible that questions will be asked, especially in the lounge bar of the Bishop & Wolf on St. Mary's in the Isles of Scilly. But the effective bluffer will soon learn to deflect these with a casual and modest: 'Oh, it's not important . . . but tell me when did you pass the 400?'

Having decided upon a list, or series of lists, the next thing to do is tick it. Ticking birds is really what birding is all about. It isn't about watching the creatures at all. All that matters is that you collect the biggest number of ticks in the shortest time, and preferably have some that your peers haven't.

Unfortunately there are rules and rules about ticking. One can't simply go through a list, pencil in hand, ticking away indiscriminately. The main reason for this is that there are certain categories of bird and not all categories are eligible.

For instance, there are birds which may have escaped from exotic collections, such as the Mandarin Duck and American Wood or Carolina Duck, some of which have hopped over the fence at Arundel's Wildfowl Trust Reserve to set up families in the lake just behind. These are known as category D birds, a motley crew which also includes tide-line corpses and so-called feral species breeding in the wild but not yet fully established.

This last little bunch includes the infamous Ring-necked Parakeet, most of the pigeons and doves you might see, and the breeding Greylag Goose. Just to complicate matters slightly, you can count Greylags in Scotland. But only in winter.

On the other hand, Category A birds, that is to say everything else, are exactly what you need for your lists. There seems to be some confusion over categories B and C – it is not clear exactly which birds fall within them, so you can safely forget them.

Dead birds can't be counted, either, unless you're in the USA. If you touch a dead bird in the US you are actually allowed to tick it. Thus a roaring trade has been established in freeze-dried rare bird corpses which iron-willed birders travel many thousands of miles to see. Fortunately, due to efficient odour-protecting freezer bags, birders rarely have to smell them as well. But in general it is best to take a strong stand on the subject of dead birds – preferably as far away as possible.

If close-ups of dead birds send US birders wild, close-ups of live birds have a more worrying effect on British birders. If the view is excellent, say in the region of from 0-6 feet, the birders are said to be crippled or to have crippling views. How this arose it is difficult to establish, but simply using the terms casually in conversation will suffice.

The flip side of crippling views is dipping, or dipping out, on some rarity. This term describes occasions when birders are unable to spot, or rather, tick the bird they have specifically gone to look for because:

a) it is playing hide and seek, or
b) it is taking an afternoon nap behind a large rock formation.

This has grown to such crisis proportions within the birding fraternity that an association has been set up especially for birders who dip regularly. The president or Big Dipper of the British Association of Dippers (BAD) defines dipping as 'succeeding in failing to see an available bird after a genuine attempt to see it'. The suggestion is that it is a useful pastime for those birders with insufficient time to go the whole hog: 'The next best thing is obviously to try and then gallantly to fail.'

Local dipping, as defined by the association, can be conducted in one's own patch – be that a back garden, a reservoir or park – while area dipping requires special skill. Here the requirement for a successful dip is to pay an abortive visit to a district noted for some particular species and then not to see it. 'To walk slowly round Loch an Eilein in the Cairngorms without seeing or hearing Crested Tits or Scottish Crossbills, for example, is a creditable double.'

As in other areas of the bird world, BAD will be awarding prizes to members that have excelled themselves in the previous 12 months. The first prize goes to the person who dips on the rarest bird of the year.

Bluffers should take dipping seriously, but not quite as seriously as mistaken identifications. One American writer once spotted a large Snowy Owl moving behind a bush while taking a class out on a field trip. Thirty eager youngsters crowded round, binoculars and telescopes all primed. Then the grass parted and out strolled a large white cat. 'I considered becoming a monk in Nepal,' said the writer. There is still hope, though, for the enthusiast. After a number of years the writer's mistake began to fade in importance, and friends and colleagues no longer pointed him out in the street or snickered behind his back. This had nothing to do with the fact that he had moved twice, changed his name and been on the receiving end of a 12-week course of plastic surgery.

Where to Watch Birders

After a few minutes' practice, the bluffer should be confident enough to try his or her hand at bluffing with a birder. This tactical exercise must be managed extremely carefully. First, you must establish exactly which kind of birder you are bluffing with and what their level of expertise is. Then you must embark on a conversation strategy, which makes it plain who is the more knowledgeable.

First there is the opening gambit: 'Anything about?' This is precisely phrased, but many bluffers get this wrong initially, paraphrasing it as 'Have you seen anything?' This is incorrect as it implies success at having seen something, something the bluffer is keen to avoid. 'Anything about?' is sufficiently vague to imply a host of things including 'What are you looking for?', 'Have you heard if there's anything about?', 'Have you called Birdline recently?' and 'Is there something that I can't quite see, perhaps hidden behind a hummock?' This last is slightly dangerous as it throws the initiative on to the birder, who may reply that there is in fact a Pectoral or Sharp-tailed Sandpiper – or some other rarity – just behind that oil drum. If the thing's asleep for the duration, as it may be on a cold day, there's no way of knowing if the story is true. (On the other hand this can be used to your own advantage when somebody asks you if there's anything about.)

Having established an opening line, the rest is more or less in the lap of the gods, but the main thing is never to show excitement, regardless of the answer – plainly you will have seen everything before: at least that's the impression you need to create. Practise saying 'Oh, really?' and 'I haven't seen one of those since yesterday at Minsmere,' with suitably demure expressions just this side of patronising, and you'll be all right. Another useful phrase for particularly rare birds is 'That'll be my first/second/third this year.'

You can bump into common or garden birders and dudes almost anywhere, but to meet the hardened twitchers, haunt the local pub. You could also make for Walberswick and other large reserves in mid-May, come the annual Bird Race; and as a last resort you could go to Fair Isle and Scilly in Autumn. These are all a bit like Daniel bearding the lion in his den, but it is worth a try if you need to improve your standing.

Public Houses and Cafés

There are a great many pubs and cafés where birders hang out to swap stories of the ones that got away and, more usually, the ones that got ringed. Some of these are key links in the chain of grapevines that supply the British birder with information on the latest sightings, so it's important to know where they are. Others, such as the Coot and Corncrake are completely fictitious, so don't get caught out.

A neat trick is to ring the best birdwatcher's haunt in Norfolk, formerly Nancy's café in Cley-next-the-Sea, but now the old coastguards' building, and ask to speak to yourself. Naturally you won't be there, but all the birdwatchers will think you're still out in the field. To imply that your service to birdwatching is above and beyond the call of duty, it's best to try this when there is at least a force 7 easterly, driving hail and sleet across East Anglia.

The other source of useful contacts can be the lounge bar of the George & Dragon, also in Cley, where the Norfolk Naturalists Trust was founded in 1926. An important sightings' record is kept here, on a lectern shaped like a large brass eagle. Do not knock this over, but look askance at anyone who does.

Perhaps the premier site for watching birders is the Isles of Scilly, which can also be called Scilly, but must never be called the Scillies or the Scilly Isles. (This makes it sound . . . well . . . silly.) The most important thing to do after disembarking from the *MV Scillonian* is to run somewhere. Make it look as if you know where some rarity is. If you're fast enough and there aren't too many people aboard, you'll be able to stop fairly soon and have lunch, or breakfast. Of course, you won't have anywhere to stay overnight because everywhere will be booked up, but that's no problem for the veteran twitcher used to cold October nights in the daffodil fields. The bluffer, however, will pay anything necessary to get a cosy room in Hugh Town, St. Mary's, preferably at the Porthcressa end.

There are a number of pubs you should be aware of in Scilly such as the Turk's Head on the quay at St. Agnes, where birders sit outside eating crab sandwiches on better days, and the Bishop & Wolf pub named after the two lighthouses, one at each end; but the important site is the Porthcressa, where log call takes place. Log call, or reporting in, is where everybody reels off:

a) the birds they've seen during the day
b) how many there were
c) where they were.

It's a good idea not to go first in the log call, you'll always be done down, but join in after a few minutes when you've gauged the mood of the meeting. Is everybody envious of the Northern Oriole on Tresco? Say you've seen two on St. Agnes.

There are some difficulties with Porthcressa in October: it's too small, and unless you're there first you'll miss the opportunity of getting a stool. It's standing room only after the first week. But it is important not to get there too early or you'll be roped into taking notes or – worse still – buying a round.

There are also logs for birders all over Scilly, but nothing like as aristocratic as the brass eagle in Cley: all the Scilly birders get are various blackboards with hastily scrawled notes. The most up to date one is generally at Longstone Centre. There is another method of finding out what's around on Scilly: simply stop someone with a CB radio and ask for Birdbrain. These sources of bird information are extremely useful to new bluffers, for a key problem on the Isles is knowing – not where all the rarities are, but where all the most famous rarities were seen. This can cause problems when you give or take directions: 'Turn left at the Black-billed Cuckoo bush' won't mean much to someone who doesn't know where the Black-billed Cuckoo was seen. You should of course use this to your advantage because no one will contradict you or ask where on earth you're talking about. If you're accosted for information just say 'It's up the hill from the Olive-backed Pipit' (unless, of course, you're already at the summit).

Scilly is also the base for pelagic seawatching trips.

Some small boats go, but on occasions the comparatively massive *Scillonian III* puts to sea, with 400 sorry birders aboard. (The birders are sorry because huge drums of chum are aboard, too. In addition to minced, rotting fish, it contains vegetable oil to help it cling and popcorn to help it float.) The general area into which the boats go is known as Wilson's Triangle. This has nothing to do with the former Labour prime minister who enjoyed holidays on Scilly, but refers to Wilson's Petrel, large numbers of which have been seen off the islands since pelagic trips became common a few years ago. Pick the right time of day, therefore, and you will find a good 500 or so birders in Wilson's Triangle, but not all of them will relish deep discussion until they're back on dry land, wrestling with a large Drambuie.

At the other end of the country, further than Orkney, but just short of the Shetlands, is Fair Isle. The island's history is long and convoluted, but as long as you mention the contributions of Eagle Clark and George Waterston no one will be able to out-bluff you. The islanders' entire purpose in life appears now to be divided equally between supporting birdwatchers, forecasting the weather and knitting jumpers. There should be no doubt which is the most important. The island can be approached by boat or plane, but both methods are dangerous. The *Good Shepherd III* (actually the island's mailboat) is much bigger than it was and it is very cheap, but in North Sea storms the effect below decks is one of having consumed a large eel. You might consider flying to Fair Isle, if only that weren't even more more likely to result in reversed peristalsis.

One of the pilots of Fair Isle's eight-seater Islander is known jocularly as the Blue Baron. On more than one occasion he is said to have waited until ten minutes after the scheduled departure time has passed before rushing out to the plane, jumping in and shouting 'Sorry, the pilot hasn't turned up – I'll have to fly.' Then, at about ten feet above the waves, 'because of the weather', he gives lucky visitors a roller coaster's eye view of the North Sea. However, things brighten up immediately on landing because Arctic Skuas nest alongside the airstrip. Don't approach too closely, though, or you'll be clipped round the ear by angry, dive-bombing parent skuas, eager to practise those last-minute turns they've seen the aircraft attempt.

Bird study on Fair Isle hasn't always been the passive scientific study it is today, as witness the occasion when the warden found a Firecrest on the island in 1981. He rushed over to one of the island's long-standing ornithologists, saying he'd found the island's first Firecrest. The dour Scot eyed him curiously and said 'Well, it isn't actually the first. I remember one sitting on that wall in October 1935, but I didn't have a gun with me so it didn't get into the record books.'

Being well on the way to Norway as it is, Fair Isle has a fair few Norse or Norn names scattered about: Mekum's Head and Sheep Craig are perhaps the best known and function as landmarks as well. Sheep Craig is a crag which, until recently, bore sheep. However, they kept falling over the edge, so the islanders reluctantly brought them down.

The centre of the Fair Isle universe is the island's majestic bird observatory – a Hilton among observatories. The garden itself and its dry stone walls have harboured many interesting migrants. One significant feature worthy of note is the lack of trees on Fair Isle. This makes life a little easier for the bluffer as the birds find it less easy to hide. To create a bit of a challenge, a small plantation – known cunningly as The Plantation – was established some years ago.

Because the island is quite small, but big enough to miss small rarities – it's three miles long by one across

– the observatory Land Rover drives round the island whenever rarities turn up, with a small red flag tied to the aerial. Drop everything and ask what's up and you're guaranteed to find where all the birders on the island are in a few short minutes.

The Orkneys, Hebrides and Shetlands also have their share of birders for the bluffer to practise on, but they comprise so many islands that they tend to spread far and wide, making any kind of group assault difficult. Orkney names end in -ay or -say: the Ronaldsays, Rousay, Papa Westray and so on, but use Hoy as your stock example as it recently recorded the world's fastest bird, the Needle-tailed Swift, clocked at 200 mph.

Where to Say You Watch Birds

Every birder has a favourite patch that he or she covers doggedly, come rain or shine, on Sunday morning just before lunch and of course every bluffer should do the same. In principle. We say in principle because the best places to cover tend to be among the smelliest, most unpleasant locations in the world. Unfortunately most bluffers don't actually do any birdwatching abroad which means that you should be familiar with the oil rigs, rubbish dumps and gravel pits of Britain.

The garden

Naturally the first ripe location for bluffing – and an ideal arena for practising the art – is the back garden, where the compost heap (formerly the rhubarb patch) has been turned into a small, ever-so wild nature reserve.

First steps towards seeing exotic birds in the garden include putting up red peanut bags for wintering Siskins (Greenfinches with black caps) and hanging one of those particularly intricate pieces of equipment that only tits are supposed to be clever enough to operate. Both are quite unlikely to have any effect whatsoever on the avifauna (birds) that appear in your garden, but if experienced bluffers are to beard birders in their own homes it is important to understand the garden regime.

Another important item is the Sparrowhawk silhouette, cut-out from black card, for the window. This in theory prevents otherwise-intelligent Sparrowhawks from flying into their own reflections and braining themselves. The most common advantage for the bluffer is as an aid for watching television. Most cut-outs are just the right size for blotting out the sun as it comes round the side of the house on a summer's day.

Garden bluffing has been made increasingly credible by the efforts of the British Trust for Ornithology/ BASF garden survey: the bluffer will not, however, send in the monthly returns because the bluffer's species list will naturally contain too many rarities for the survey to consider seriously. However, in public, bluffers should hold the scheme in high esteem.

Nesting boxes are another item that sets the bluffer's garden apart. At least two varieties of box should be hung – with small holes for tits and open-fronted for Pied Flycatchers. It's also important to put an old shoe up on a post, or place a kettle on its side (in full view, of course) for all those Robins that pass through. If you have a leaking roof that you never quite get round to fixing, it's also a good bluff to put a Swift nesting box in the loft. This kills two birds with one stone, so to speak. You can impress other birders with your dedication and have a good excuse for not fixing the roof at the same time.

Those whose householders include a tortoise should get into the habit of making jokes about the local Lammergeier, an evil-looking vulture, which takes our shell-encased friends to a great height only to throw them at the ground – very hard. (NB This is not funny if you live in the Middle East or southern parts of Europe, where the 1.2 metre Lammergeier makes its home.)

Top Gardens

1. Mr & Mrs Smith (name-changed) in the pretty Surrey-town of Christmas Pie, whose kitchen and garden still bear the scars of hundreds of birders trooping through to see a visiting Rose-coloured Starling. Their experience bears re-telling as it's common enough in certain locations, such as the Isles of Scilly. Mr Smith was coming home from the shops when he spotted some chap skulking in the undergrowth, staring into the house with binoculars. Taking the fellow aside, Mr Smith found him to be mostly harmless, and agreed to let the birder contact the telephone information service Birdline, divulging the whereabouts of the Starling. This was the Smiths' biggest mistake. By the following morning – and for days afterwards – they were suffering siege conditions.

2. No mention of gardens would be complete without describing the weird and wonderful delights of that famous garden on Fair Isle, captured forever in a recent book. For the ardent birder this book is heartbreaking – describing the arrival of strange warblers and pipits, as well as less usual garden birds such as Petrels and Red-footed Falcon.

3. Vicars' gardens everywhere: Hoopoes.

4. The Forest Lodge in Abernethy Forest offers the most remarkable opportunities for bluffing in the Cairngorms. Who will believe your stories of those parties of Capercaillies displaying manically on the

lawn in Spring? Bluffers should sigh, reminiscing openly about memories of the old days; for the 100-strong flocks have long gone. You would be in good company, however, if you reported that you failed to see them, or dipped. (It's always a good idea to show some humility – listeners are even more likely to believe your next tale.) Sassenach birders who've never ventured north of Hadrian's Wall are far more likely to believe your fleeting glimpse of the Scottish Crossbill, Britain's only home-grown (use the word 'endemic') bird. Describe a small band skeetering across the tops of the pines alongside Loch an Eilein and watch the nods of agreement, approbation and – best of all – envy.

5. Tunnicliffe's house, Anglesey. The home of this famous bird artist is now a small hotel. Talk about the migration of birds up the Irish Sea, and don't forget that you can see the Isle of Man on a clear day.

6. Lord Dashwood's garden. Strictly speaking this is not really a garden, but a gravel pit. The full reasoning behind the creation of the pit is long and somewhat perplexing, but it would seem that Lord Dashwood started the now-infamous Hellfire Club in the latter part of last century and he excavated large pits in the Buckinghamshire countryside to hold its black masses and Witch/Warlock orgies. The situation has changed since then and the only thing that anyone sees there now is the Cirl Bunting – Buckinghamshire provides one of its last strongholds.

Top Sewage Farms

Sewage farms have been under a great deal of pressure recently, as various water authorities in Britain have been modernising facilities and introducing new technology. Replacing the old sludge pools or sewage lagoons with gravel circles and sprinklers has been drastic. No self-respecting wader is going to be seen ankle deep in gravel, neither will it be forced to hop over a rotating sprinkler arm every few seconds.

This in turn means birders will soon lose interest in sewage farms, which can only make the bluffer's life more pleasant. You must never admit this, but publicly hanker after more and smellier sewage farms. 'I've-done-it-all' bluffers should tell of slippery escarpments and near misses at sewage farms, but the truly dedicated will actually do the decent thing and fall in.

At Beddington SF in Surrey the heaps of earth being moved continually from one side to the other provide useful vantage points from which you can occasionally see Lesser Yellowlegs on the lagoons. Wisbech SF in Cambridgeshire used to be good for various sandpipers, but in recent years all has come to naught. Tring in Hertfordshire is actually more famous for its reservoirs, but the bluffer will nod sagely letting it be known that the sewage farm is much better, especially since they made room at the front for car parking. Summer specialities include Garganey and Ruddy Duck.

Top Reservoirs

Reservoirs tend to be a little flat, but can hold a few rarities, especially after gales at sea. The bluffing conservationist birder (not as difficult a task as you might think) should denounce local councils which allow water sports on reservoirs. First it frightens the waterfowl, but the biggest problem is that watching grown adults trying to keep their windsurf boards upright is a real hoot and distracts from the more serious pastime in hand.

Farmoor Reservoir in Oxfordshire is known in its day to have sported a Leach's Petrel (a long, long way from home), but the discerning bluffer will throw doubt on the sighting, suggesting it must have been confused with a House Martin. Another good vagrant here is the Grey Phalarope (Red Phalarope in the US), which marched up and down the shore, in and out of the yachts and yachtspersons preparing for a big race. Clearly this inquisitive individual had no idea it was supposed to be somewhere else.

Staines Reservoir in Middlesex is actually only one of a number of reservoirs, but birding officials keep some of them – and thus the rarities – to themselves. In company, mention how cold it gets in the winter, especially when you're raised up on the central walkway. Wait for the sympathy when you relate the meteorological quirks of the county which mean there's always a sharp north easterly across the water, whatever the weather in Staines itself. Staines has one big problem: it's directly beneath 93 flight paths of the adjacent Heathrow Airport. Despite the noise strange grebes – such as Slavonian and Black-necked – are a speciality here, which leads one to suppose that their ear tufts actually function as muffs.

As for Rutland Water in Leicestershire – first, always claim it is in Rutland; second, claim it as the biggest reservoir in Britain and that you've walked every foot of the west bank's nine-mile shoreline.

If you're a 'glutton-for-punishment' bluffer, you could always state you'd walked the other 27-odd miles, too. (Ignore claims that Strangford Lough is bigger. Offer the argument, kindly, that Strangford doesn't count really since it's in Ireland.) Mentioning the near-ish Blithfield and Eyebrook Reservoirs gains you credibility as an expert on the Midlands, but don't forget also to mention the lakes at Ellesmere in Shropshire. It doesn't matter that you can't find them on the map.

At Avon's Chew Valley Lake, Herriott's Bridge is, naturally, the best place for bird and wildlife – Bitterns have even been seen ice skating (Bambi-style) on the frozen lake in hard weather. But the important thing to bring to any fellow birders' notice is the clever way the reservoir is called a lake, making it sound much more natural. Take care not to run down the other local reservoirs, Cheddar and Blagdon, as the West Country folk are very possessive of them.

The most famous of all reservoirs in Britain are the Tring Reservoirs in Hertfordshire, steeped in ornithological history, much of which is now water under the bridge. The important things to remember are that Tring was the (former) home of the Great Crested Grebe and of Sir Julian Huxley (a top bluffer). Here it was that the beleaguered Great Crested Grebe was saved from extinction in the 19th century. However, don't go to Tring looking for Great Crested Grebes now, as they've pretty much moved on, as has the British Trust for Ornithology, which set up its headquarters in Tring to look after them.

Never visit on Sundays or Saturdays or Bank Holidays because of The Public, who insist on coming along in their thousands to see the views (Chiltern Scarp, Chiltern Hundreds) and to eat Mr Squidgee's ice cream.

Top Nuclear Power Stations

Power stations, for some strange reason, always seem to attract birds; nuclear power stations especially so. (There is a belief among some bird experts that it's the less intelligent birds that gad about nuclear reactors – the sensible ones keep away. The same could be said for bluffers.)

Whether it's the heat or the smell or the noise no one is quite certain, but Black Redstarts are fond of big square concrete buildings, as are many migrant arrivals. The surrounding coastal dunes often hide Wrynecks and shrikes of various kinds, but the key point at any power station is the hot spot, always known as 'the patch'. This is not the reactor itself, but a point on the sea beside the station where hot water is pumped out into the ocean. This hot water attracts a variety of marine lifeforms, which in turn attracts unusual gulls and terns.

Sizewell in Suffolk is quite usefully placed, being a few miles south of the RSPB's Minsmere reserve (but don't mention Sizewell B in conversation). Other stations worth a visit all begin with the letter H and can be remembered by the simple mnemonic: Hurricanes hardly ever happen in Heysham, Hinckley and Hartlepool. Hartlepool offers the chance of seeing a Chilean Flamingo – salmon pink, vermillion and black. It escaped from a nearby collection some years ago and occasionally drops by to feed, preen and rest. A second, paler bird has also been spotted, but it vanished on a cold day one January, taking with it the vision of future generations of homegrown Hartlepool flamingos.

Top Car Parks

Perhaps the best place to watch birds is from Britain's car parks. This is amazingly good value for the bluffer, who simply arrives, winds down the window and clamps on the 'scope. No hides, no walking, no aggravating questions from lesser beings.

At the car park by the Wells end of Holkham Meals, a three mile conifer plantation in Norfolk, rare Parrot Crossbills have nested in the tree tops. But to the amazement of the RSPB warden set to guard the nests day and night, the loving parents would – in broad daylight, with plenty of people milling about – fly down to puddles near the ice cream van to scoop up water for a pine-needle paste.

The even rarer Indigo Bunting has been seen here, too, but so far there has been no correlation with ice cream, of whatever taste or colour.

1) Epsom Downs car park.
Excellent for Lesser-spotted Woodpecker. The others are here, too, but don't expect to see them.

2) Leighton Moss RSPB reserve.
You can't quite see Bittern from the car park, but you can hear them. You can however see Blackcap and Marsh Tit, as well as a host of other small songsters.

3) Cairn Gorm Ski Lift car park.
At about 750 metres above sea level Red Grouse is easy here. In the depths of winter Ptarmigan is a possibility, but the landowners have cunningly placed big white rocks all over the mountain side making identification quite difficult. This prolongs the observation process, generally inducing frostbite, which can be cured by copious quantities of coffee and hot chocolate at the co-incidentally named Ptarmigan Café – just short of the summit.

4) Cley-next-the-Sea car park, Norfolk.
Suffice to say that the powers that be have even built a hide at the car park at Cley. This creates the impression that absolutely anything can be seen absolutely anywhere in Cley. Which is probably true.

5) Church Wood car park, Kent.
Roding Woodcock are common at dusk, while the commoner Nuthatch and Woodpeckers are almost impossible to see without actually going into the wood. It is possible to hear Nightingales, a Kentish speciality, but don't claim to see them often: no one will believe you.

6) Church Norton car park, West Sussex.
Firecrests and Wrynecks have been seen at this famous car park, and you can tell if shrikes, particularly the Red-backed variety, have been about when you see collections of small insects and birds impaled

on thorn bushes.

7) Minsmere RSPB car park.
Sand Martins nest in the car park and white-rumped Hen Harriers have been seen on their way through, hawking various members of the more unlucky bird species. Black Redstarts are common, too, around the flagpole. (NB: The regular appearance of the Black Redstart does not mean Minsmere is a nuclear power station, only that Sizewell is too close for comfort.)

8) Arundel Wildfowl Trust car park.
As at any collection, fence hoppers can always be seen, and Arundel car park is no exception. In general, fence hoppers are frowned upon by birders, but Arundel's Mandarin and American Wood or Carolina Duck are doing very well, thank you, across the road on the Swanbourne Lake.

9) Dinas RSPB car park, Wales.
This car park is amazing in that Garden Warblers can actually be SEEN, flitting from one side to the other, warbling away to their heart's content. Until his visit to Dinas, at least one birder had in fact been placed in the invidious position of having walked all round a small bush in which a Garden Warbler was singing – to no avail. It was invisible.

10) Ashdown Forest Centre car park, Kent.
All kinds of birdlife here including, though rare, Lady Amherst's Pheasant. Ashdown Forest is perhaps more famous as the setting for *Winnie-the-Pooh*, and owls are still a possibility.

Top Hides

Hides in the birdwatching context refer to small wooden sheds, some with small slits for windows and benches, others with big glass windows and central heating. There are no prizes for guessing which the bluffer deplores publicly, but secretly enjoys the most.

Top hides in order of precedence are:

1. Welney Wildfowl Trust Main Hide.
The most luxurious in the UK is the big, tilted windowed, centrally heated hide on the banks of the Old Bedford River. It must, of course, be castigated and defamed by the bluffer in public, who should wear a scowl inside the hide for appearance's sake. The 'better' hides at Welney are tiny two-person affairs in plastic or glass fibre, embedded in the mud and ooze. Bluffers over six feet tall with no wish to contort themselves painfully have an instant get out – basically because they can't get in.

2. Peng Observatory at Slimbridge Wildfowl Trust.
Not to be outdone by that upstart Welney, the WT's headquarters has upgraded its Swan Lake hides with the addition of a picture-window, centrally heated hide, too. It has established a new trend by calling it an 'observatory'. There are other 'observatories' – at Holme and Sandwich to name but two – but none of them are as warm in winter as this one. An advantage of Slimbridge over Welney is that you can study flamingos while tackling soup and rolls at the café.

3. Minsmere Island Mere Hide, Leighton Moss Lower Hide and Loch Garten Osprey Hide.
Although less luxurious than the Wildfowl Trust Hides, these RSPB hides give stunning views of birds including the elusive Bittern and Water Rail. No points for guessing where you see nesting Ospreys.

4. Wilmore Reservoir, Tring.
This has to be the most street-credible hide on the list, constructed only from a sheet of corrugated iron

propped up with lengths of 2x4. However, by peeking cautiously around it you can get stunning views of the ever-amusing Ruddy Duck display. Don't try to pass the hide off as credible in the company of maniacs – they don't use hides.

Twitchers' Havens

Some of the more dangerous places for the bluffer are where the world's twitchers spend most of their time: at the corners of Britain. These people are ruthless and will catch you out and cut you down without a moment's hesitation. It is important, therefore, to practise bluffing before you try your hand in these locations.

The twitching world is divided over which corner of Britain is the tops, so it's best to fall into one camp or the other: Scilly or Fair Isle. They're both pretty good so it doesn't matter which (unless you're Scottish).

When to Watch Birds

There are basically two times of day to watch birds:

1. night time
2. daytime.

Daytime is easiest. There is, however, a variety of birds that occupies the dim zones between night and day – dawn and dusk – and these birds have become known as crepuscular, since it sounds more impressive than twilight.

We would normally suggest you didn't bother with any nocturnal activities, such as Nightjar hunting, that take up valuable free time, but as drinking hours have been extended to cover the entire day, bluffers can feel a little less guilty now.

Nocturnal birding can be difficult, but the bluffer

should be reassured by the fact that – even for serious birders – it tends to be done by accident. There is the by-now famous winter's night story of Mrs McCreadie (name changed), who, while practising three-point turns on her Aviemore farm, using forward and reverse gears in the time-honoured fashion, saw, in her rear view mirror, the top foot or so of a fence post turn round and fly off. When she regained consciousness, the driving instructor explained that Barn Owls always sat on fence posts like that before flying off, 'ghostly white, into the inky night'.

At dawn and dusk, crepuscular birds are what you're after. Or – if you're sensible – not so much after, as seriously avoiding. These sneaky birds are either very timid creatures, hiding at the first sound of human company, or they're very cunning, out to catch tired prey. The Woodcock is a typical crepuscular sort, only waking up at these split-shift times to zoom around its favourite wood, sometimes roding in the trees for the benefit of female Woodcock.

The final and most important category for the bluffer includes the daytime or diurnal birds. The word diurnal, although meaning in or of the day, is usually twinned with the phrase 'birds of prey', so the honest bluffer should never separate the two. There are quite a few diurnal birds of prey, so the phrase is a useful catch-all. Beware the temptation to use the phrase 'nocturnal birds of prey'; these are usually called owls for short.

Daytime itself presents a problem, as it changes constantly throughout the year, but the best time for birds is always early in the morning, i.e. just after dawn. This is positively the worst time for the bluffer, always last to leave the pub the night before, telling the most fantastic stories of crippling views of Great White Pelicans (not in St. James's Park, either). The following timetable should help give you some idea of the times to report early morning activities:

Season	Dawn	Activities to report
Spring	5-7am	Dawn chorus gets louder.
Summer	3-5am	Dawn chorus loudest ever. (Black Grouses lek, Capercaillies go into trances.)
Autumn	6-8am	Dawn chorus almost non-existent. (Parents hide nest location to protect young.)
Winter	7-9am	Dawn chorus feeble. (Sparrows get up even later than the average bluffer.)

There is a modicum of activity everywhere after dawn for about two hours as everyone shuffles round for breakfast. Seawatching is good for about two hours after dawn, especially during Spring and Autumn migration, the chief passage periods.

A bit further into the day, but equally confusing for the inland bluffer, is the relationship of wader activity to the tide. Essentially waders run about quite prominently for two hours before high tide, then they vanish for hours on end. Low tide on the other hand is absolutely hopeless for waders – they're bound to be on the distant shimmering mudflats seven miles out to sea. Holme dunes, for example, seems like a wader exclusion zone at low tide.

This tidal activity is complicated further by the appearance of neap tides and tides which ebb or flow, but as it is far too complicated to remember whether flowing or ebbing is coming or going it is safest for the bluffer to ignore time and tide all together and go to a sewage farm.

Seasonal Birding

Mention seasonal birding to the inexperienced and all they'll think of is a Christmas turkey. The quick witted bluffer will appreciate that birds spend some time flying into and out of the country and that it tends to happen at set times of year. This activity is responsible for small birds being known as migrants.

Spring is perhaps the best passage period, with many thousands of birds coming to summer in Britain. Having reached these shores (no mean feat in itself, navigating by starlight), these summer visitors commence a detailed schedule of complex biological processes, such as moulting (some quickly, some slowly, some more than once) and mating (ditto).

In the summer, the birds that are here should all be settling down to family life. Things are still pretty vibrant in the wood, though, in May, when hordes of mad people spend an entire weekend on a 24-hour bird race collecting as many ticks as possible. A lot of famous birders can be seen on this day, but don't interrupt asking for autographs – every second counts.

In the height of summer, you can legitimately take a holiday at the seaside, as all the seabirds such as auks and terns are nesting on ledges and cliffs, or indeed on the beach itself. It's a pretty noisy time – and if you get too close to those oil-spitting Fulmars, it can be pretty nasty, too. The official twitcher's line on summer is that on the whole it's a complete washout as there aren't too many vagrant waifs and strays being blown to our shores. Fortunately, summer never lasts long in Britain and Autumn is soon on its way, bringing back the first winter birds, or indeed migrants that are just passing through.

As a practising bluffer, you should be aware that September is peak activity time on Fair Isle, while Scilly gets busy in October. Booking accommodation in either resort is difficult, to say the least – the Fair

Isle hostelry, for instance, can be booked up for years. You could admit that you haven't been to one or the other site for humility's sake, but as most bluffers have no humility you may as well fib like all the rest.

Once the autumn passage begins, moulting also commences. There are a number of reasons for moulting, but in the main it boils down to puberty or improving the aerodynamics ready for the return trip. Moulting into the often more drab winter plumage can take some time, especially for larger waterfowl, and duck such as Eider tend to gather in large flocks, or rafts, on the water as they lose the power of flight. Moulting males tend to look just like females, so before opening conversation with another birder about the surprising number of females around, think again. Some will be that bane of the birder's life, the so-called eclipse males.

As winter draws on apace, the geese and swans start to return. In conversation you should mention the Svaalbard population of Barnacles at Caerlaverock and mutter about the shooting of White-fronts on Islay. There is always the chance of a Snow Goose, too, at this time, but if someone claims to have seen one at Stranraer throw cold water on the sighting by saying it's bound to be feral.

January 1 is a traditional day out for birders and bluffers everywhere, as they button up their overcoats for their first sightings of the year, more often than not sponsored for the BTO or the RSPB or some such organisation. You can probably expect to count thirty or so species on this first day without trying too hard – you may even manage it from your garden if you put out a few stale mince pies. Hardier bluffers will of course get the car out – despite the temptation to sleep off the New Year's Eve festivities – and head into the country with the left-overs. At least then, if it's positively too cold to get out of the car, you've got some emergency rations to keep your strength up.

THE BIRDS

The most unimportant aspect of birdwatching is, of course, the birds themselves. Before contemplating some of the less dull specimens, consider the extremely complex business of names.

The traditional or common names for most birds were created by country folk or, in the case of seabirds, sometimes by fishermen. The booming Bittern suffered most at their hands, coming away with names including Bumble, Mire Drumble, Bitter Bump, Butter Bump, Buttle Bump, Bottle Bump, Bog Blutter and Bull o' the Bog.

Habits and appearance have also been predominant factors in the christening of many species, for example Cherry Sucker for the Spotted Flycatcher and Heather Bleat for the Snipe. Others are onomatopoeic (Cuckoo, for instance), or commemorative, defining forever the first discoverer of a bird.

Scientific names consist generally of two or three parts:

1. the genus or generic name
2. the species or specific name, and if you're really unlucky –
3. a sub-species or sub-specific name.

When all two (or three) are the same, this suggests that what you've got is a pretty typical example of a pretty typical species of a certain genus. Try using *Troglodytes troglodytes troglodytes* – the Wren – the longest latin name for the second smallest British bird.

For those students of Latin and Greek, the derivation of some scientific names is puzzling, because the genders or constructions are frequently incorrect. This is because the people who, in history, have been responsible for naming birds were all bluffers.

Perhaps the easiest scientific name to memorise is *Puffinus puffinus puffinus*. But don't be fooled into thinking that this bird is a Puffin; it's not even an atypical Puffin. It's a Manx Shearwater: a slim-winged, seagull-type bird, brown above, with a narrow, less-than-colourful beak. (Anything less like a Puffin you couldn't find in a hurry.) However, the 19th century birder who first extracted a Manx Shearwater fledgling from a burrow and ringed it thought it was a Puffin chick, and thus it is recorded for all time.

If you think the *Puffinus* saga is extraordinary, consider the Swedish naturalist largely responsible for the entire scientific naming procedure. (He did not actually name the birds, though; he cribbed most of it from Pliny and we all know what happened to him.) First, his name was Carl von Linne, but he became famous only when he was known as Linnaeus. Secondly, this naturalist – intelligent though he was – actually thought that ducks and drakes were separate species, and gave them separate names. Until he saw some of them mating, that is. (Bluffers of all kinds, take heart.)

Someone beloved of all list-makers is K.H. Voous, whose 1977 list has been adopted by most ornithological associations as the standard for British birds. (Why he couldn't put them all in alphabetical order is a wonder most bluffers soon learn to live with.) But more changes are set to come. The Records Committee of the British Ornithologists Union (BOURC), responsible for maintaining the British List has submitted provisional name changes, to harmonise with the US and the EEC. Bluffers should either reject these outright or adopt them all. There is no middle path.

Some of the more disagreeable name revisions include the proposed demolition of the name Andalusian Hemipode (effectively a flying tortoise) for replacement as a Striped Button-Quail; Stone Curlew will become Northern Thick-knee; Dunnock (or Hedge Sparrow) will become a Hedge Accentor; and, worst of all, the good-old Bearded Tit will become a Bearded Parrotbill. There is a series of grammatical changes, too, including hyphen additions (Dark Chanting Goshawk to Dark Chanting-Goshawk) and word splits (Woodlark to Wood Lark), whose purpose remains unclear.

Divers

These are the most primitive bird species seen in Britain and only notable because they occur first in all the guide books and can be found instantly. (Thank Voous.) The best is the White-billed Diver but, in its absence, the Great Northern Diver will do as a good bluff, especially if you describe it in its summer plumage at Loch Fleet, say. These birds all make crazed and manic noises when breeding, which has resulted in their being known in the US as Loons.

Cormorants

These all-black birds are memorable because they stand on rocks with their wings outstretched. (Quite why, no one knows, so make up your own theory.) The slightly-smaller Shag is thought to be a candidate for the Loch Ness monster.

Swans and Geese

Mute Swans are the largest and most common, but they're certainly not mute. They can be told in flight by their noisy wings and on the ground by their knobbly bills. They hiss and honk, too, often giving forth a twangy trumpeting note. Never get too close to their cygnets, though, unless you want a nip somewhere nasty. Despite the niceness of the Mute, the bluffer should be more interested in the Bewick's and Whooper Swans, and espouse the cause of the Wildfowl

Trust Swan Supporter Scheme. Joining this entitles you to a big diagram of all the different types of beak.

Svaalbard is worth mentioning as the summer home of Caerlaverock's Barnacle Geese, but never say how wonderful they are to the islanders of Islay, who have to endure some 20,000 of them for the entire winter.

The other geese are all grey and pretty much of a muchness, except for the black and white Canada Goose, which you should deride as feral.

Ducks

There is a problem in the name game as far as ducks are concerned: a duck is a female waterfowl (males are drakes), but there is also a whole category of birds known as ducks, some with the word Duck in their name, such as Mandarin Duck. This can lead to some confusion: 'There's a Mandarin Duck duck over there, ducking behind the Wood Duck duck.'

The Mallard is of course the archetypal duck as it goes quack. (No other duck does this.) The second best known 'duck' is in fact not a duck at all, but a Coot.

The smallest duck is the Teal, with a large green, teardrop-shaped eyestripe. But don't be confused by the slightly larger Garganey, which has a white eyestripe. Other pretty common ducks, but worth a mention, include the whistling Wigeon and the growling Gadwall. The drake Pintail – as its name suggests – has a long thin tail and is often regarded as many birders' personal favourite because it's pretty.

In general, ducks can be divided into two groups: dabbling or diving. Those above are dabblers. Divers include another common duck, the black and white freshwater Tufted Duck, which looks more or less like the marine Scaup with a tuft, while the Pochard can be distinguished from both by its red head.

Seaducks

You should declare all distant black seaducks to be Velvet Scoter, never the more common Common Scoter, while small black and white ducks will be Long-tailed Ducks. (Note, however, that only some will have long tails.)

All big brown ducks will be female Eider, except during moulting periods when there will be males there, too. Male Eiders in summer plumage are big, white and black with a greenish neck. It's impossible to miss them not only because of their plumage but also because of their head-wobbling display and 'very interested' ooooOOOOoooo call.

Sawbills

There is a tendency among birders to call females of most sawbills (and some ducks) 'redheads'. Female Red-breasted Mergansers (seagoing Goosanders) also have red heads, as do female Smew (and Goldeneye, apparently). This can be confusing, though, as some immature males have redheads, too. So on practical (as well as sexist) grounds, the practice should be avoided by the enlightened bluffer.

Birds of Prey

It is best to describe these as diurnal birds of prey or, better still, raptors. Raptors come in three basic sizes – small, medium and large – and their plumage details are incredibly complex, never seeming to stay the same from one field guide to the next.

Small raptors are characterised by the hovering Kestrel and the Swift-chasing Hobby, while medium-sized raptors include the Hen and soaring Marsh Harriers. (Hen Harriers offer another Duck saga, as you can have cock Hen Harriers – try not to confuse yourself.) At the top end of the spectrum are vultures (thankfully not in Britain) and eagles (sadly not common in

Britain).

True birders get quite animated about raptors, especially when seen at great distances over forests or reed beds, silhouetted against a glowering sky, or shimmering through a heat haze. This might sound as if raptor watching is rather difficult, with the elements and the environment conspiring against you. Not so. It's the easiest thing in the world for the canny bluffer to get by in, provided you heed the following cautionary tale.

Two inexperienced birders, one might even say dudes, on their first outing to the phragmites (or reed beds) of Stodmarsh in Kent, were raptor watching. A small party gathered halfway along the main path and suddenly someone drew attention to a movement on the horizon. The dudes raised their cheap bins to their eyes and scanned the horizon. Nothing. 'It's either a Hen, a Montagu's or a small Marsh,' said the bluffer, as the alleged bird – which no one else saw – got slightly closer. Still no sign in the dude's bins, despite frantic pointings and fumbling with field guides.

The bird, we imagine, twisted in mid-air and late afternoon rays of sunshine glanced off its back and head. 'It's a Marsh Harrier,' said the bluffer, with the right degree of certainty in his voice, 'and it's an adult male.' The dudes threw down their bins in disgust and were flicking through the field guide helplessly as the bluffer moved off. As soon as he was out of earshot one dude turned to the other and squeezed through gritted teeth: 'I can't believe that guy;' (the dudes were American) 'I couldn't even find that bird and he could see its genitals.'

The identification was of course based on imaginary plumage characteristics, not on visible organs. The dudes had clearly never seen an expert in action before.

Most medium-large raptors are buzzards of one kind

or another, only distinguishable by plumage. If you find yourself in the company of someone who claims to see a Honey or Rough-legged Buzzard, it's best to throw doubt on the sighting ('Why, isn't it a buzzard?'). You're pretty safe with this as Buzzards pass through almost all British airspace.

Some vagrant raptors do occur, which are a welcome diversion. An American Bald-headed Eagle, way off-course, fuelled excitement recently, as has the secret breeding success of the White-tailed Sea Eagle. But THE raptor is the Golden Eagle seen only in the Cairngorms and latterly in the English Lake District. The best way to see a Golden Eagle is to find a mountain and climb it. Failing that, bluff as best you can. This bird is having a huge revival of fortunes among birders, who at one time thought them ten a penny, so they're always a good thing to bluff about seeing these days. (However, if the eagle poisoning goes on much longer in the Scottish Highlands, everyone will have to bluff about seeing the bird because there won't be any living specimens left.)

Game Birds

Most game birds were introduced for sport, so it's best not to treat them too seriously. When the various birds are 'in-season' (Grouse from the 'Glorious' 12th of June) it's best to regard these as off limits. It can actually be quite dangerous stalking these birds because hunters know no boundaries.

When in Europe, however, bear in mind that there is no close season, despite official appearances. It may also be worth reminding the overseas bluffer that continental Europeans have a rather unwelcoming attitude to terrorists, so mock flak jackets are a mistake.

There are a number of problems with game birds: because so many closely related species have been set loose, they have started inter-breeding. Red-legged

Partridges and various kinds of Chukar are now providing birders with hours of heartache. The bluffer should forget all these. There are enough problems with grouse, without adding more.

The Red Grouse, which is brown, not red, appears up mountains above about 1500 feet, but can be seen lower down if the weather is bad. The male Black Grouse is easy to distinguish (it's black) but the female is a problem – it's brown, like the Red Grouse. The female Capercaillie is bigger, but looks much the same again as a Red Grouse, while the male is best seen entranced in the Spring.

Waders

These are generally characterised by long, spindly legs and long thin bills – usually downward curving, though some cause confusion in the field by pointing upwards. The Redshank is perhaps the archetypal wader, with long red legs (hence the name) and a long, albeit straight, bill. This is much the same as its cousin, the Spotted Redshank (which also has red legs, but is black with white spots), and its second cousin, the Greenshank (which has green legs). So far, so good.

The Ringed Plover is nothing like the archetypal wader. It is tubby with short legs and a short straight bill. It does however have a black ring round its neck and forehead and can't be mistaken for any other species. (Except a Little Ringed Plover. This is almost exactly the same, but smaller.)

Some of the longest legs in the wading world belong to the aptly-named Black-winged Stilt, but the most famous wader is the Avocet, whose upwardly pointing bill has become immortalised on half a million RSPB car stickers.

Probably the most complex bird in the entire avifauna is the Dunlin. This bird is so common and ordinary it has to be seen (numerous times) to be believed.

Its vague brown-ness and widely variable size (5-8ins) mean it is capable – in the rarity-starved mind of the birder – of impromptu impersonations of almost any small wader, especially rare American vagrants such as the Pectoral Sandpiper. In any randomly-selected bunch of 30 birders you can guarantee that no fewer than 30 will describe this bird as something else.

One final wader is the Ruff . . . or Reeve. Not only do the two sexes have different names (thanks to our old friend Linneaus), they can range from 8 to 12 inches in size and have almost any colour plumage. (The birds offer a number of colours in the leg department, too.)

Other reasonably common waders to look out for are the godwits, about 15in from tail to long straight bill. The godwit with the longest legs is called a Black-tailed Godwit, while the godwit with medium-sized legs is called a Bar-tailed Godwit. The Godwit with short legs is actually not a godwit at all, but a Snipe. (But if you see a Snipe in a wood, at twilight, it's probably the crepuscular Woodcock. Simple really.)

Seabirds

As all bluffers know, there is no such thing as a sea-gull. There are, however, gulls in all shapes and sizes. Most of them are all white to a degree, which makes them relatively easy to distinguish in the field, but they have different coloured legs and beaks, which complicates matters. Some – like the appropriately named Black-headed Gull – have black balaclavas in summer. Good gulls to travel miles to see include the Glaucous and Mediterranean Gull, though there are certain individuals who can be relied upon to turn up in the same place year after year. These individuals tend to be named after a while and perhaps the most famous Glaucous Gull was called George. (Be warned that the Common Gull isn't common.)

Birds that you might mistake for small, slim gulls are in fact terns – Arctic, Common and Sandwich, mainly – and what you might think of as large gulls are in fact albatrosses. The only real albatross you might possibly expect is the Black-browed Albatross, a rare visitor from the South Atlantic. Bluffers may like to try mimicing the cry: Gah, Gah, Gah. This goes down very well in the pub.

If seabirds look like brown gulls, they are probably skuas. These are pretty mean individuals that generally chase other birds. They are often described as pirates of the open sea, causing other species – Kittiwakes and Puffins, for example – to regurgitate their last meal, part digested for ease of use.

Other common seabirds are contained in the auk family, which look like flying Havana cigars. It's almost impossible to tell these birds apart at any distance and you can safely call any black flying torpedo you see a Guillemot, a Black Guillemot (or Tystie for credibility's sake) or a Razorbill. Smaller cigars – a cheroot, perhaps – will always be a Little Auk. Puffins are also auks, but these can easily be told by their big clown faces and coloured beaks. It is generally considered uncouth to like this charming comedian of the cliffside: but you're allowed to have a soft spot for it.

Warblers

The birds in the British list that currently generate the most excitement, are also the most dreary. These are the warblers – generally small brown jobs, very unspectacular. Perhaps it's the identification challenge, but these are the ones that really fire the twitcher.

There are a number of basic warblers, which the new bluffer will soon learn to deal with. The Chiff Chaff, for example, which looks like a Willow Warbler, conveniently sings the phrase 'Chiff Chaff' repeatedly. The Willow Warbler, on the other hand, looks like a Chiff Chaff, but doesn't say so.

The slightly rarer Blackcap (male) has a black cap, but note that the female and juvenile who have brown caps, are still called Blackcaps.

The Sedge Warbler is perfect for the bluffer: it likes sitting in reeds making a demented mixture of mechanical and melodious sounds. It has a nice big identifying eye stripe, unlike the Reed Warbler, which also sits in reeds, but has no eye stripe. This latter bird, however, sounds like a squeaky toy sitting in the reeds. The Marsh Warbler, in comparision, only sits in reeds at a particular section of one river in the West Midlands. Forget it.

The Wood Warbler is large and yellow and sounds like a clockwork toy sneezing, while the Dartford Warbler (the conservationists' favourite) is notable principally because it is threatened by fires and destruction of its native heathlands. (Beware: this bird cannot be found in Dartford.)

The distinguishing feature of the Garden Warbler is that is has no distinguishing feature. It loves being invisible. The Grasshopper Warbler is also more likely to be heard than seen, churring away like a grasshopper. This differs from the Savi's Warbler which makes a deeper grasshopper-like sound. Cetti's Warbler is distinguished only by the fact that it was named after an Italian.

Never hesitate to claim that you've seen Pallas's Warbler, Pallas's Grasshopper Warbler, Pallas's Rosefinch and Pallas's Sandgrouse for good measure. (NB: Pallas's Sandgrouse is not a warbler, but it was first seen by Pallas, who as a young man worked very hard at finding new birds.) It's also worth throwing into the conversation odd facts such as you found a Radde's or Dusky Warbler once ('and aren't they getting common these days?').

Tits

One of the commonest and most well-loved garden birds is the Blue Tit, but its larger cousin, the Great Tit, is the one that causes the bluffer problems. The Great Tit has something over 50 different calls and birding in a spring woodland can be a trial. 'What's that?' you might say and spend the next half hour tracking only to find yourself nose to beak with a Great Tit. The loudest cry from the undergrowth is, however, that of the Wren. Perhaps its loud call is nature's way of compensation for its machismo factor of nil.

The Blue Tit's country cousin is the Coal Tit, which is like a brown Blue tit, with a black head and a white patch at the back of the neck. Things are complicated slightly by the Marsh Tit (a Coal Tit without the white patch, that sings 'Pitchuu Pitchuu'). Thankfully, most birders don't take tits too seriously. The two exceptions are the Crested Tit (a Coal Tit with a crest) and the Bearded Tit, which sounds like an old-fashioned cash register and isn't actually a tit at all.

Buntings and Finches

The general birding opinion of the common species is 'worthy but dull'. The Chaffinch is the most common finch, indeed one of the most common birds altogether, but how anyone can render its call as 'Cricketer cricketer cricketer, running to wicket, bowling' is difficult to imagine. Don't report seeing Hawfinches too often; few birders will believe you.

Reed Buntings have a plaintive 'Please keep clear' song, but perhaps the most famous bunting call is 'A little bit of bread and NO cheese' from the Yellowhammer. How it can abide singing this for hours on end is understandable only to other Yellowhammers.

Crows

Crows are characterised by being all black, intelligent and generally at the back of field guides. There are, however, exceptions. If the Crow is the archetypal crow, then the Hooded Crow is a crow in a short-sleeved pullover. There is also the Rook (a crow with a white bill), the Jackdaw (a small crow with a grey nape), and the Chough (a red-legged crow that says 'Chough'). The Magpie (a long-tailed black and white crow) is thoroughly disliked because it eats other bird's chicks, so you could take up its cause in the interests of humanity.

Perhaps the most widely known crow is the Raven whose extraordinary ability to count is hampered by the fact that it can only reach five. For this reason you need six people to sneak up on the Raven, five of whom then depart (noisily) leaving one person to get a perfect view. Make sure it's you.

Sex

Sex lies behind all the multifarious hues, patterns, songs and shapes in the bird world and is therefore a subject that cannot be discreetly or decently ignored. Britain has its fair share of eccentric avian behaviour, but the most outlandish and bizarre rituals are only really to be witnessed in distant, exotic locations. These being extremely difficult and expensive places to get to, a well-placed, throwaway remark about the time you had a crippling view of the rarely-witnessed courtship ritual of Australia's Superb Lyrebird will enhance your reputation immensely. And few people will be able to contradict you.

For those not familiar with the fine detail of the lyrebird's lovelife, here is a summary of the main points to mention. The lyrebird is normally a very ordinary brown and grey bird, resembling a rather drab female Pheasant. When pitching the woo, however, the male lyrebird overcomes his physical dullness with a dazzling display. First he clears a stage for his performance, either building a hummock (Superb Lyrebird) or digging a three foot crater (Albert's Lyrebird). He then moves centre stage and launches into a vast repertoire of song, throwing in the odd impression of other bird species for good measure. After a few minutes, he starts to unfold his magnificent tail, which is far longer than the rest of his body and generally shaped like a lyre, with two outer feathers forming a colourful U-shape around a mass of thin, gossamer-like feathers that compose the lyre strings. He then tilts this tail right over his head and obscures his unexciting body completely from view. The act is designed to mislead the female lyrebird in to thinking he's the most desirable creature in creation.

In addition to courtship rituals, there are other sexual phenomena with which you should be familiar.

Violence

Sex and violence is inextricably intertwined in the bird world. Most violence is restricted to defending territory or their young: the males of many bird species lay claim to a piece of land, which they defend from other birds of the same species – and sometimes from other species or lifeforms too – with a great deal of vigour, whether it be no more than a few feet square, or in the case of an eagle, a goodly part of a mountain range.

Birds usually advertise their ownership of a particular tract by singing, hence the popular harmonies of the Blackbird or the Nightingale. Their vocal expertise can also help to attract a mate, which tends to be quite useful for sex.

The bluffer is advised to decry the use of tape-recorded bird song to entice a species of bird to sing and hence reveal itself – some birds are frightened off by the sudden arrival of such impressive competition in their territories and never return. However, if a true, rather than tape-recorded, rival dares to enter another bird's territory, this can provoke all manner of feigned or real fights. Male ruddy ducks, for example, go in for posturing, sticking their tails in the air, bobbing their heads and making quantities of bubbles, before chasing off an intruder at breakneck speed and apparently trying to bite his tail. Capercaillies – normally shy, retiring birds – will attack anything that moves, including human beings. Woe betide, too, the innocent bluffer who goes to sees the cute baby Eider Ducks at Walney Island, near Barrow in Furness, without a bamboo pole with a feather stuck on the end of it.

The speciality act of the huge colonies of Herring and Lesser Black-Backed Gulls is diving, in their hundreds at unprotected human heads, with as much force as possible. And then defecating on them. Even more frightening are the attentions paid to intruders by the Great Skua, known as the Bonxie. Fearless birders claim they never actually hit you, but bluffers are advised not to risk it just in case.

Colours and Display

As in the case of the lyrebird, bright colours are useful when trying to show yourself off in a dark jungle. A suitably sensational place to say you've witnessed the advantage of colour and ritual in the procreation of a species is New Guinea, where the male Birds of Paradise deck themselves in gold, iridescent blue and metallic green and dance themselves into a frenzy – all in the cause of attracting a mate and outperforming any other males (a bit like John Travolta in *Saturday Night Fever*). Other birds with impressive wooing routines include the Great Bustard, which turns itself into a large feathery puffball on legs; the Magnificent

Frigate Bird, which inflates a red balloon under its chin; and the Ruff, a wader that can be almost any colour it chooses and grows a huge ruff of feathers around its neck to impress the Reeve.

Other notable and original performers include the roding Woodcock, the Black Grouse with its lek and the Tree Pipit with its parachute flight. There is also the Capercaillie, which struts his stuff on the branch of a tree, points his bill to the sky and emits an amazing string of grating, slurring, coughing, and hissing sounds. While he does so, he becomes deaf to the world, which is rather unfortunate as hunters can sneak up and shoot him in mid-performance (an act that at one time led to the virtual extinction of the species).

Nests

The most impressive constructions of the bird world are not in fact nests at all, but treasure houses constructed by the Bowerbirds. Where most birds are content to throw a few twigs together, the Bowerbird builds palaces and stately homes. New Guinea is again a good place to see these structures, which consist of large huts built around saplings, usually decked with moss carpets and filled with brilliant orchids, shining beetle wings, bright berries and colourful pebbles. Some species of Bowerbird, being particularly DIY actually decorate the walls, too. The bowers are unfortunately much more impressive than the birds that build them. Equally sadly, the females do not consider the bowers as suitable places to bring up a family and usually fly off to construct a more practical nest elsewhere leaving the male to act as caretaker.

The Weaver Birds are similarly notable architects, some of which live in communal blocks of flats, and the Wren and Blackcap, who go to the trouble of building several different nests only one of which will the female choose to live in.

BIRD PARAPHERNALIA

The human race has been writing about and painting pictures of birds for many hundreds of years – thousands of years if you include cave paintings. Most of the paintings made late last century and earlier this century by giants such as Thos Bewick, Geo Edwards, C.G. Finch-Davies (truly) and John James Audubon were portraits of dead birds. Indeed Audubon thought that his day was not worthwhile unless he had shot over 100. Bluffers may truthfully declare that the reason Audubon's birds have such contorted poses is that he insisted on drawing them life size, and was thus compelled to fit pigeon and pelican within the largest possible page (known as double elephant).

Not many know that the Scots traveller Alexander Wilson, after whom Wilson's Petrel is named, fled to America after being convicted for blackmail. From hunter and trapper of birds he soon became a painter and publisher, proving an inspiration to the more-famous Audubon.

In this enlightened age, bird books are illustrated by birders just as maniacal as twitchers themselves. Chief among field guide writers is the US author Roger Tory Peterson, who started the whole idea of putting tiny pictures of birds on one page and describing them on the other, tagging on a collection of minute distribution maps at the back. Quite why all the birds face the same way is not certain, and there are those birders who insist they can only identify species if they adopt the correct orientation in the field. This is a useful excuse, but not particularly versatile. The active bluffer should be able to run round the other side of a bush or tree containing a prominent rarity. (This doesn't help with birds at sea, however.) Publishers are now beginning to realise that birds can be seen both ways round and most modern field guides show the avifauna in a useful mixture of poses.

As usual in academic circles, books are known by the collection of their co-authors' names. Thus there is Peterson, Mountford and Hollom for the traditionalist, or – for the more broad-minded – Heinzel, Fitter and Parslow. Some bluffers should, however, swear by Ferguson-Lees, Willis and Sharrock, even though it's difficult to pronounce quickly. The reason that the books have three authors each is easy: one writes, one draws and one maps. The practice of identifying books by their authors is a useful means of distinguishing between field guides, which all tend to be called *Birds of Britain and Europe* or some variation on this theme.

If the name Sharrock doesn't ring any bells at present, it should be chiselled in stone for the bird bluffer. Dr J.T.R. Sharrock is the Managing Editor of that most essential of monthlies, *British Birds*. This sets the pace for serious detailed information in the bird publications world, but the young upstart *Twitching* (now *Birding World*) has its followers, too.

The existence of the modern field guide is strange because the twitching fraternity has effectively put paid to their use as an instant reference work by frowning on birders who need to refer to books in public. In private, though, they take a fanantical delight in owning as many guides and books as possible and this is another area where the bluffer can score points.

One book that is very definitely not a field guide is the literally massive *Birds of the Western Palearctic*. This is so big it comes in volumes, each a veritable giant in the publishing world, written by tens of people (which is why the book is known as BWP and not by its authors).

Would-be birders should aim to be perfectionists. One of the methods you can use, for instance, to distinguish between the different bird books is to consider the style of bird naming. Some authorities, including the RSPB, spell bird names with lower case letters, thus: little ringed plover. Many others, however, think this is confusing, and use capital initial letters: Great Black-backed Gull. Bluffers should fall firmly on one side or the other and refuse to have anything to do with those in the other camp.

Another kind of bird book that has grown in popularity over the past few years is the 'I know there are some birds out there, but where on earth do I find them?' variety. John Gooders effectively kicked off this scene with his *Where to watch birds in Britain* and latterly *Ditto Europe*.

In the past few decades professional bird photography has also attracted attention and names such as Hugh Clark (how did he get those pictures of the woodpecker?), Bruce Campbell and Eric Hosking (now one-eyed courtesy of an irate owl) should be littered freely in any discussions on photography.

In addition to books about birds, there are a great deal of recordings of bird noises, made by such famous figures as Ludwig Koch, H.F. Witherby and James Fisher.

The BBC has most recently released a record of birds in stereo, but the bluffer should suggest that surely the thing you want most from a recording is for the source to stay put. Birds are difficult enough to listen to in reality without more lifelike (i.e. moving) recordings. The idea of bird calls and song on a record or tape, to help identify species, is brilliant, but the trouble with long-playing records is that after a while the brain tires, and then the only thing you hear regularly is the voice of the announcer. One bluffer in the George & Dragon at Cley was overheard to say the only thing he felt he could identify readily from bird recordings was Eric Simms.

BLUFF YOUR WAY ABROAD

In the USA, birding is much easier than in the UK, largely because there are far more birds and home-grown birders can't keep track of all of them.

Places to go in North America include the Everglades in Florida (complain about the alligators under the car) and the Yukon Delta in Alaska. This 200-mile wide delta offers the largest wildfowl refuge in the USA. It's the breeding ground for Cackling Canada Geese and for Pacific White-fronts and the Emperor Goose. (It's important to hire a boat and take plenty of money in case of emergencies. And because the place is so big, a personal stereo probably wouldn't be a bad idea, either.)

Geese are also prevalent on the Spanish Coto Donana: up to 30,000 Greylag Geese fly round in massive skeins, while twice as many Wigeon dabble round their feet.

The gorgeous Rift Valley lakes are the Cley of Kenya – Lake Nakuru is eight miles long by four wide with a flamingo population of one to two million. At a mere 25 miles from the equator and 6,000 feet above sea level, you would be wise to take a beany hat. As well as keeping off the sun (perhaps), it may afford a little protection against the somewhat aggressive White-headed African Fish Eagle. But don't bank on it.

If you like waterfowl (and water) try Bharatpur just south west of Agra, India, during the monsoon. There, a steaming freshwater swamp occupies over 1,000 hectares between July and September. The history of this man-made reserve is closely linked to the whims of the Maharajah of Bharatpur, who originally planned it as a shooting complex until someone pointed out money could be made from conservation, too.

But the best place in the whole of the world is . . . (write your answer here).

GLOSSARY

Crippled/crippling – With excellent views of birds one is said to be crippled. The source is difficult to establish, but the effect is suitably graphic.

Dude – A well-to-do birder with some real knowledge, but not a lot.

Eclipse – An eclipse male is a drake duck in the process of moulting. A godsend to the bluffer who can safely point to any female duck in late summer and claim it's an eclipse.

Greenie – A budding birder with expensive gear.

Gripped off – If a colleague claims to have seen an American Bittern or a Ring-billed Gull and you haven't, consider yourself gripped off or jealous. This sounds painful. It is.

Hide – a) The preserved skin of an animal; b) any contraption for secretly observing birds (US = blind); c) what the bluffer should do if he or she actually gets the urge to watch birds.

Lek/lekking – The dance of the male Black Grouse. This is invariably held (a) by the side of the road, and (b) early in the morning when no self-respecting bluffer is about.

Maniac – The kind of birder you wouldn't want to meet in a light alley.

Passerines – Anything not covered by sensible names such as gulls, ducks, etc. A catch-all category often defined as perching birds.

Roding – The practice of the Woodcock in mapping out his territory with a display flight. Silly, really.

Twitcher – The archetypal birdwatcher.

THE BLUFFER'S GUIDES

Planned or in preparation:

Architecture
Banking
Beliefs
The Classics
Contemporary Cinema
Defence
Espionage
Finance
Gambling
High Society
Law
Modern Art
Opera
Politics
Psychology
Public Relations
Seduction
Selling
Ski-ing
Travel
World Affairs

The USA
The Australians
The British
The French
The Germans

Amsterdam
Berlin
Hong Kong
Moscow
New York